R e s e m b l a n c e /與

Jonathan C Chou

Distributed by Independent Publishers Group
Chicago

Saturnalia Books
2816 North Kent Rd.
Broomall, PA 19008
info@saturnaliabooks.com

ISBN: 9781947817746 (print), 9781947817753 (ebook)
Library of Congress Control Number: 2024935292

Distributed by:
Independent Publishing Group
814 N. Franklin St.
Chicago, IL 60610
800-888-4741

獻 給

周 震 世

張 仙 芬

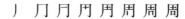

丿 刀 月 冈 冏 周 周 周

CONTENTS

Three Cameras
5

1947 | 2021
17

□
25

Where I find myself standing before a ruin
43

I
60

Notes
65

THREE CAMERAS

Stolen symbols for

Instead of a pet, my father bought us a point-and-shoot camera from 光華商場 where he used to go with friends a lanky unathletic young man sporting the aviators of the time my knowledge of coming from the few photos my mother kept. See him there killing time marveling electronics. Then the latest in the Canon PowerShot IXUS series, in retrospect it was considered compact by every standard. Too enthralled to dissect, still through instinct a body invents systems to manipulate.

My hand feels the way it tells me this is an IXUS.

Integrated technologies and advanced electronics build an array of beautifully styled and precision optics. The 4.0 Megapixel sensor allows. The 3x optical zoom delivers heritage culminating in corner-to-corner clarity while the 9-point AiAF ensures off-center subjects even. Performance demands plenty of processing power is why Canon's dedicated DIGIC processor is a hidden photographer's assistant. The Intelligent Orientation Sensor rotates images for playback. With sound recording and "in-camera" editing, Manual mode is perfect for creative control. Connecting camera to printer and pushing the Print/Share button speeds up online sharing to any Windows PC. Create instant photo prints or a series of movie clip frames.

In quadrangles found mirrors now memories of

天母

Winded trees cast shadow branches upon a cracked wall. The Great Wall Plastic Factory was the first manufacturer of the Diana a toy factory in Kowloon, Hong Kong, established in 1955 in baby blue so as to appeal amateurs. A case containing twelve dozen sold whole for 50¢/unit. The industrial arts supplies importer Power Sales Company of Willow Grove, Pennsylvania, received. According to the *Encyclopedia of Twentieth-Century Photography*, like us it traveled under other names: Anny, Arrow, Arrow Flash, Asiana, Banier, Banner, Colorflash Deluxe, Debonair, Diana Deluxe, Diane F, Dionne F2, Dories, Flocon RF, Hi-Flash, Justen, Lina, Lina S, Mark L, MegoMatic, Merit Mirage, Pnanx Photon 120, Pioneer, Raleigh, Reliance, Rosko, Rover, See, Shakeys, Stellar, Stellar Flash, Tina, Traceflex, Truview, Valiant, Windsor, Zip, and Zodiac over time multiplicity yields to an empty frame no mystery we feel adrift

It was intended a cut rate consolation

He learned to aim one fingerbreadth to the left to take account the trajectory. The shutter opens. By cicada sound feel heat of summer stolen moments for alleyroaming what does a dream feel like

塑膠 hands 塑膠 head 塑膠 body 塑膠 eyes 塑膠 hair 塑膠 feet 塑膠 organs 塑膠 blood 塑膠 brain

They were there together where. Past is known by memory of warmth the substitute of one sun for another. Returning he noted the absence of wings the still surface of sky the difference in his vision

With bodies we make vectors to the world

Port of entry
   He makes a crumple of it all. The car sputters.

   Benefit Street, Prospect Street, Brown Street, Thayer Street, Brook Street, Hope Street, Cooke Street, Governer Street, Meeting Street, Angell Street, Waterman Street, College Street, George Street, Benevolent Street, Charlesfield Street, Power Street, Williams Street, John Street, Arnold Street, Transit Street, Sheldon Street, Wickenden Street.

   For many the quaintness of New England turns out quite the convincing image of bliss. In its original form the contrast of numerals in gold leaf with the wrought iron fence was felt great. Or in old buildings reading old books where pretense means holding the Great Works of the Western World in mind like a fat stool a well-rounded education in the theory of shapes and ethereal real world applications figures merit. What of myths and traditions that rely on a sense of belonging where there is none translates to business as usual including clandestine since 1869 when *Liber Brunensis* was founded for publishing membership lists of the vaunted secret societies first without senior portraits per Martha Mitchell's *Encyclopedia Brunoniana* until 1896 then the era of albumen silver prints made with hens' eggs and silver nitrate which rendered in sharp the unsmiling faces of all white men except one Black guy from Mystic so putting a face to the racism of the time so to speak later I become assistant photo editor then photo editor of this esteemed vehicle of history. In time a word's letters take shape in the world to define what is and is beyond us but even chains can be broken out of so if true that the unconscious is structured like a language then lack is to be found in an optical experience and the possibility of saying what it is to be a them in language lies in the visual. I am talking about reclaiming the diasporic subject and the penchant for pleasure and bad behavior which unite the poet and the crook. I took off after the fact and now all that remains was. The subject in every case is my pleasure.

the frieze the theft the fractal

of 與 for
metonymy 與 metaphor
alienate 與 separate
stereotype 與 subjugate
identity 與 disparity
history 與 historicize
myth 與 retelling
possess 與 surrender
belong 與 concord

control which is shown the locu
how English obstructs every a
linearity encounters recursivity in

s of reduplication not the margin
ttempt I make to articulate
an image I have seen before

H   I   R   I   N   G

The taste of Chinatown Resonates within me

百 食 不 膩 ASIAN CRAFTS 回味無窮

is one of PHANTOM'S "GREAT ATE" for

Activating   blood   stasis   Solutions

E   X   O   T   I   C   EMPIRE GARDEN

C   O   C   K   T   A   I   L   S

N   E   W   J   U   M   B   O   S   E   A   F   O   O   D

Quench your thirst   THE AUTHENTIC TASTE OF

O   r   i   e   n   t   a   l   t   h   e   r   a   p   y

Matcha-licious   しゃぶしゃぶ

Mind your body   Connie's Beauty Center

B o d y   s l i m   税   t r e a t m e n t

湊一起，省更多   W h i t e n i n g

We   Do   Jewelry   Repair

More Phone   AS MEDICAL OFF E   More Fun

hungrypanda.co   se habla español

Original Sichuan Cuisine   Trans 環

TIỆM VẢI NỮ-TRANG   Pacific

The   feeling   every   Travel 美

body wants   just "look past the dingy

dining room" and "admire 最大的障礙是語言

+BOBA   the efficiency" of the staff."

One   day   you'll   find   a   house

that   could   be   a   home.

Vancouver + Rocky Mountains

瓊   安   介   紹   所

E   A   S   T   W   E   S   T

T   A   T   U   N   G

M   E   G   A   S   A   L   E

1947 | 2021

a nation's consciousness blooms from a field of graves the silhouettes of heads like headstones. I look upon them look with them my kith and kin. It is the darkness awakening in each which

is the dead friend? When in medical school I learn the deceptiveness of bullet wounds the devastation caused within which cannot be forgotten

unable to see we make do with mythology

in Alhambra Greataunt tells me that her brother-in-law my mother's uncle was there his friend or was it his brother was shot dead and he went retrieved the body from the smoke filled streets

and went mad

the path in is overgrown
and lost easily still it leads

jamais vu: when in words the spaces between letters open into sky yawning to engulf. Memory coheres as loosely and empty corners whisper of obsolescence

lost to time

a thick smoke obscures. They watch as he is drawn in. In the dark in the distance two ghostly sails rise up. The flaming pile takes center stage what comes from grief what flickers. The dead hide their faces the tens of thousands what is not seen is felt indelibly. The permanent dislocation captured in the estimate is

not the image
but its incomprehensibility
inherited. The failure of ekphrasis is the knife cutting through time

19

on the way to the station we said little. Years were waited and you had moved on. The umbrella lay cracked in the wet street and the stars which had guided were dreamt up

street cleaning every Thursday

at face value everything was as it had been. You estimated the time it would take us to get back

it was not just a matter of timing. The question had always been how to say nothing. Finally we stopped looking for a way out

was as it should be

like wax reforming in the sudden dark the shapes words take betray a movement
of stars

what stung caresses
solace found in loss

you were there even when

noticed then that the watch
had stopped working. I had attempted to tell you everything. The new door
swung open both ways and the broken glass was not picked up. We were
contented to fail fail again

our mail makes a small pile on the kitchen counter. You and I have a number
of loose ends in common

we look for each other through the aisles

the flowers you photographed are in my car still

□

Army of Chang Kai-Shek executing Taiwanese citizens in 1947

what is accessible is the sense of
having been created by moments

    that   have no memory of

but the sounds that came out

    were not words

        but their opposite

There is a straightforward meaning to what is depicted but not here or the way they appear like actors upon a stage where I seek nation and find distance

What is revealed is how we are born into all prior obscurations or choosing to keep history silent the dead lie flat on the ground or silence history

The stadium erupted in cheers and was heard a distant roar that shuddered when on that day the clouds came in from all directions or his is poetry recited from the margins

I watch from the window as they drive off or what spans every distance is the yearning so the photograph is a symbol of or I am the emptiness howling across generations

偷偷

What a wave is is a question about the ocean or   They left empty-handed and
he gazed at the bird soar

暗流

My parents dreams of a distant   Where corners stand empty a home becomes
the form time takes   We spoke from rooms to time   It is dark in still we feel
each

舞文

A garment hung up recalls the warmth of a body even   There would be no difference between them under the new law   Or: glimpses of you in the interstices

全家福

He awoke one morning to discover his arm no longer part of his   It would not utter   We face them to them

When asked by reporters why the narration of the Keelung harbor shooting was voiced over or in view of or footage of the Shanghai massacre in the program, Chen said that "the narration did not match the images," but she implied that this did not amount to fabrication nonetheless

from received forms new
shoots reach sky toward

and journalism tries to cover its tracks.

"Viewers must be thinking that the video images portrayed what actually happened is what actually happened is what actually happened during the 228 Incident because the program did not indicate otherwise is the childhood home we left behind for distance; the reporting was obviously a case of

移
花
接
木

and thereby misleading the viewers," the report said while poetry flashed its seams.

"We didn't
fabricate
the special report.
We didn't
know
and Juan
didn't inform us
of the fact.

the clip
was about
the civil war
between the KMT
and the CCP.
Nor did
she write it
in the letter

There was
no indication
on
the master
tape,
of authorization
,"
Chen said.

Hu Yu-wei, professor of National Taiwan Normal University's Graduate Institute of Mass Communication, echoed Lin's view,

the chamber was built to be heard
(invasion)

saying that the sensitivity of the 228 Incident requires

extra   caution
straight   shot
docile   missile
corpus   replica

in the production of reports. "The audio should match the images, and unrelated pictures should never be used," he stressed

and sky closes as quickly.

Political commentators on the Talking Show last night threw the blame on field coordinates to mirror the opposition KMT for a mutual weaponization, saying shell fragments that a near diffusion of light eclipses and the party was the one attribute to nothing fabricating the truth of the 228 Incident.

At a press conference yesterday, KMT Legislator Hung Hsiu-chu said:

"There is a saying that
when a lie is told

1,000 times, it becomes
a truth. This was

the subjugation
is etched into

SET-TV's motive
for the special report –

a silence more brutal
than imaginable

to make people think
of the KMT when

the brutal image
comes to mind."

"We want to thank SET-TV for making the special report on the 228 Incident. While the image was not about the 228 Incident, many   people were killed in exactly the same way as that shown in the film."

WHERE I FIND MYSELF STANDING
BEFORE A RUIN

A page is torn from the historical record

The failure to capture the dimensions of any given moment in time through sequential acts of delimitation defines a psychic experience of density

Wild animals are drawn to the site where speech was   They no longer dreamed
of those cities

When on his journey he discovers markings the shape of but not
theirs   Unravel paths the lengths of oceans in search of

She followed grief across in search of second mothers   The images that were
lost on the way over

He arrived at the decision to paint nothing   It was nothing anyway that could
be put down

New words were needed for living

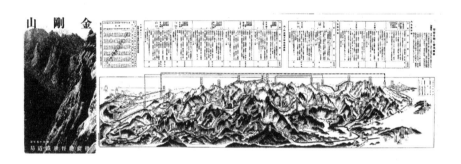

It is not what is said that endures   It is not a bridge that connects us but a
series of missed calls

The barren trees outside his window where once birds flocked cast shadows over
the page of his hands

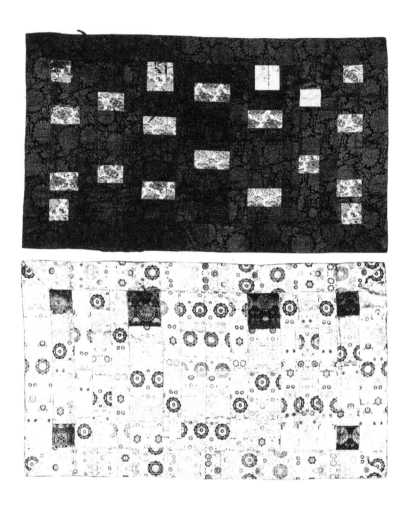

This is a poetry of physical ideas or the patchwork mountains where we wander
till we feel home

Rain falls until an ocean   We dream until sleep

How we stutter still over our names

I

周
刀
土
口

masts   sisters

FROM THE SECRET ATLAS OF THE EAST INDIA COMPANY, c.1670

words in the shape of forts

ruins built from blueprint by loaned hands

Photograph of a Street in Chinatown at Nighttime

the embrace of artifacts

GATE I. SECTION I. TIER D. NICHE 33.

From many I have come to resemble. "Three Cameras" borrows its form from Susan Howe's "Frame Structures." "1947 | 2021" is indebted to Theresa Hak Kyung Cha's *Dictee*. "I" is written after Myung Mi Kim.

Sources for "Three Cameras" are: "Canon IXUS 430 / Powershot Digital ELPH S410 4.0MP Digital Camera - Silver," eBay, https://www.ebay.com/p/100218893; Lynne Warren, *Encyclopedia of Twentieth-Century Photography*, New York: Routledge, 2005; and Martha Mitchell, "Liber Brunensis," *Encyclopedia Brunoniana*, Providence: Brown University Library, 1993. Page 15 is collaged from billboards, commercial shop signs, advertisements, and other elements of the linguistic landscape seen from street level in Boston's Chinatown in February 2021. The photograph on pages 20 and 21 was taken by an unknown photographer on February 28, 1947, in Taipei, Taiwan; the image belongs to the public domain.

The image that appears on page 26 is used as the cover image for the Medium article "'228 Incident' a precursor of life in America? Or a cure for our stasis?" (Millstein, 2020), where it was first encountered. The text on page 27 is from the caption. Other sources for "□" are: Hermia Lin, "SET TV criticized for attributing incorrect footage to 228 Incident," *Taiwan News*, May 9, 2007; Flora Wang & Shih Hsiu-Chuan, "KMT slams SET-TV over documentary," *Taipei Times*, May 9, 2007; Shih Hsiu-Chuan & Flora Wang, "KMT politicizing SET-TV 228 footage issue: DPP," *Taipei Times*, May 10, 2007; and "The 228 Massacre - 60 years on, Part 1/3" uploaded by Tim Maddog, March 1, 2007, https://www.youtube.com/watch?v=k77bl5jP4Jo (links to Parts 2 and 3 in video description).

The images found on page 3 and in "Where I find myself standing before a ruin" are from the following sources (in the public domain):

P. 3: [Curlyrnd], "Los Angeles Chinatown - General Store 3," 2022. Digital copy licensed under CC BY-SA 4.0. https://creativecommons.org/licenses/by-sa/4.0/deed.en
P. 45: Carleton Watkins, "Trestle on Central Pacific Railroad," 1880, J. Paul Getty Museum.
P. 46: Wang Zhiyuan after Huang Shang, "T'ien wên t'u [A Map of the Stars]," 1247.
P. 47: F.C. Wieder & Martinus Nijhoff Publishers, "Taioan, Formosa. - From the Secret Atlas of the East India Company, c.1670," 1925, National Library of Australia.
Pp. 48-49: J. D. Givens, "Immigration station, Angel Island, Cal.," c. 1915, Library of Congress.
P. 50: Dorothea Lange, "San Francisco, California. Families of two Shinto priests who were interned on December 8, 1942, im…," 1942, U.S. National Archives and Records Administration.
Pages 51-52: Jirka Matousek, "Alishan Mountain Range, Taiwan," 2023, Flickr. Digital copy licensed under CC BY 2.0. https://creativecommons.org/licenses/by/2.0/
P. 53: "Kumgangsan," 1939, Geographicus Rare Antique Maps.
P. 54: [Tsaokayez], "HK Central Piers 中環碼頭 interior window shadow," 2010. Digital copy licensed under CC BY-SA 3.0. https://creativecommons.org/licenses/by-sa/3.0/deed.en
P. 55: "Brocade, silk. A Buddhist monk's robe: Kesa" & "Brocade, silk. A Buddhist monk's robe, patched; kesa," Edo Period, National Museum of Asian Art.
Pp. 56-57: [chih12], "cosmos--@I-Lan Park," 2005, Flickr. Digital copy licensed under CC BY 2.0. https://creativecommons.org/licenses/by/2.0

Jonathan C Chou is the author of *Resemblance/與*, winner of the 2023 Alma Book Award. His writing has appeared in *Synapsis: A Health Humanities Journal, The Healing Muse,* and elsewhere. He teaches in the Master of Science in Narrative Medicine at the Keck School of Medicine of the University of Southern California and is completing an MFA in Creative Writing at Antioch University.

*Resemblance/*與 is printed in Times New Roman
www.saturnaliabooks.org